Contents

D1307762

Introduction

The charming creatures in *Cupcake Whimsy* are all about fun. However, they are also a little *unusual*. They come in fanciful colors complete with funky stripes or spots, some have googly eyes, others are sporting enormous ears and goofy mouths. They may be strange, but they are very cute!

Cute is just one of the reasons to add *Cupcake Whimsy* to your cookbook collection (and its companion book *It's a Cupcake Party!* by the same authors). *Cupcake Whimsy* features 12 cupcakes and toppers with 4 interchangeable recipes and 6 yummy frosting variations, and most include a secret tasty filling that's sure to be a surprise. All 12 are crowned with fun and imaginative toppers made with fondant.

Cupcake Whimsy

Text and Photography by
ELISABETH ANTOINE AND ELIZABETH CUNNINGHAM HERRING

SELLERS
PUBLISHING

To my wonderful children, Basile and Eloise,
inspired I am by their endless creativity.
—Elisabeth Antoine

To my husband, Rich, and my two
sweet little cupcakes, Olivia and Isabelle.
—Elizabeth Cunningham Herring

Acknowledgments

We would like to thank our friends and families for their support and for being our cupcake guinea pigs! Tasting the cupcakes was lots of fun, but it may not have been the best thing for our diets.

We would especially like to thank Greg Tobin and Edward Ash-Milby for their advice, and Julie Pauly, Wendy Foster, Kat Lozynsky, and Caroline Cunningham for all their help.

We would also like to thank our agent, Coleen O'Shea, and our publisher, Robin Haywood, for their encouragement and support.

Published by Sellers Publishing, Inc.
Text and photography copyright © 2012 Elisabeth Antoine & Elizabeth Cunningham Herring
All rights reserved.

Sellers Publishing, Inc.
161 John Roberts Road, South Portland, Maine 04106
Visit our Web site: www.sellerspublishing.com
E-mail: rsp@rsvp.com

ISBN 13: 978-1-4162-0689-7
e-ISBN: 978-1-4162-0732-0
Library of Congress Control Number: 2011935332

How to Fill a Cupcake

Like the whimsical creatures that top them, most of the cupcakes in this book feature something a bit unexpected — a tasty filling such as lemon curd or chocolate pudding that complements the flavor of the cupcake and adds a little zing.

With a knife, cut a small circular hole in the top of the cupcake.

Pull out the cutout center.

Fill the hole with the selected filling. Make sure not to overfill.

Carefully frost over the top of the cupcake.

When finished, your cupcake should look like this. No one will know there's a secret buried inside.

Fondant Fundamentals

A key ingredient in many wedding and other specialty cakes, fondant is a truly amazing substance. It's easy to use, versatile, and can be used to create remarkable sculptures without any kind of special equipment.

Fondant is a very sweet concoction. Though our recipe calls for corn syrup, you can substitute honey for a slightly healthier version. Please keep in mind that the corn syrup called for is the one used in most pecan pie recipes, not the highly processed high-fructose corn syrup that has received a lot of negative attention lately.

That said, we find that commercial fondant is smoother and much easier to use than the homemade variety. In fact, the toppers in this book were all created using commercial fondant. Fondant is available in many different colors. However, we suggest using white fondant and adding food coloring.

Following are some tips to follow when working with fondant:

- After adding food coloring, knead the fondant until the color is evenly blended and you have achieved your desired shade. If you are using gel food coloring (our product of choice), you may want to wear plastic gloves during this process to avoid rainbow-colored hands for the rest of the day. It is better to make a little more of each color than you think you'll need, as it may be hard to match the color if you want to use it later.

- As fondant can sometimes stick to surfaces, place parchment paper under the fondant as you work.

- If necessary, you can use a tiny bit of water to "glue" pieces of fondant together. For example, if you need to affix an eye to a figure, and it doesn't seem to be sticking, dip a toothpick in some water and use that to "glue" the eye on.

- When not working with the fondant, place it in a zippered plastic bag or airtight container until you are ready to use it. If stored properly at room temperature, commercial (not homemade) fondant will last for 18 months.

- The fondant toppers can be made up to 2 days ahead. Store them in a cake storage container or on a lightly covered tray at room temperature. (In a more humid climate, you may want to store them in a cool, dry place.)

- Whatever you do, do not store the fondant toppers in the refrigerator or freezer, as this will cause them to get soft and shiny. You should also avoid storing the finished fondant toppers in an airtight container or bag, as this will have a similar effect. It's important that the container not be airtight; you want air to circulate to keep the fondant from drooping.

- For best results, do not place the finished toppers on the cupcakes until you are ready to serve them.

Homemade Fondant
(makes enough for 12 to 18 cupcake toppers)

⅓ cup hot water
⅓ cup light corn syrup (Karo) or honey
5–6 cups confectioners' sugar

Mix together the hot water and corn syrup or honey. Quickly blend in 5 cups confectioners' sugar until smooth. Knead the fondant, adding small amounts of confectioners' sugar until it forms a dough-like ball and doesn't stick to your fingers.

Keep the fondant in an airtight container to avoid drying. If the fondant gets sticky, feel free to knead some more confectioners' sugar into it.

Spacy Alien

Devil's Food Cupcakes with Vanilla Buttercream Frosting
and Raspberry Jam Filling

We don't think our stargazing Spacy Alien could frighten a fly — in
fact, he makes E.T. look scary! He's guarding a delicious secret
surprise in his cupcake spaceship, but he may be willing to share!

Makes 18 cupcakes.

INGREDIENTS

For the Cupcakes:

3 ounces unsweetened
   chocolate

$1/2$ cup unsalted butter

2 cups packed dark brown
   sugar

2 large eggs

2 teaspoons vanilla extract

2 cups all-purpose flour

2 teaspoons baking soda

Pinch of salt

$1/2$ cup buttermilk

1 cup boiling water

For the Frosting:

1 cup unsalted butter,
   softened

1 teaspoon vanilla extract

4 cups confectioners' sugar

2 teaspoons milk

For the Filling:

Raspberry jam

Preheat oven to 350°F (180°C). Place 18 baking cups in 2
muffin pans.

Melt chocolate and butter together in a double boiler. In a large bowl, stir together the melted chocolate mixture with the sugar. Add the eggs and vanilla and mix until well blended. In a small bowl, mix the flour, baking soda, and salt. Add about half the flour mixture to the chocolate batter, then add the buttermilk, and then the rest of the flour mixture. Stir gently with a wooden spoon until well blended. Add the boiling water and stir.

Pour the batter into cupcake liners until they are about two-thirds full and bake in the center of the oven for about 20 minutes or until a wooden toothpick inserted in the center of a cupcake comes out clean. Cool on rack for 30 minutes before frosting. Store unfrosted cupcakes in an airtight container in the refrigerator for up to 3 days.

For the Frosting:

Cream butter with an electric mixer in a large bowl. Add vanilla and then gradually add sugar, beating well and scraping the sides of the bowl. Add milk and beat until light and fluffy. Store in the refrigerator until ready to frost the cupcakes. If the frosting gets too hard, let it sit out at room temperature until it's soft enough to spread. The frosting can be stored in a sealed container in the refrigerator for up to 2 days.

Before frosting the cupcakes, fill them with the raspberry jam. See page 5 for filling instructions.

You will need:

- Fondant in the following colors: light green, dark green, white, black
- Butter knife
- Toothpick

1.

Spread frosting evenly over the filled cupcake.

2.

With light green fondant, make an olive-shaped body.

3. Using more light green fondant, make 2 petal-shaped feet.

4. Place the feet under the body and place the body on top of the cupcake.

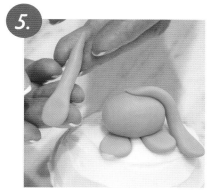

5.

With more light green fondant, create 2 inch-long arms and flatten the ends to form hands. Attach arms to the top of the body.

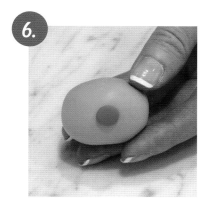

6.

For the head, take a larger piece of light green fondant and roll it into an olive shape. Use a little ball of dark green fondant to create a mouth.

7.

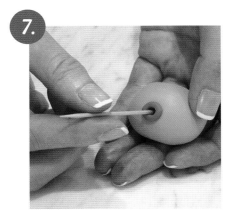

With a toothpick, create an opening in the mouth.

8.

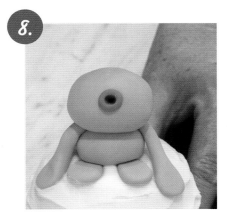

Carefully place the head on top of the alien's body.

9.

Take 2 small balls of light green fondant, flatten them, and roll them to create the alien's tubular ears.

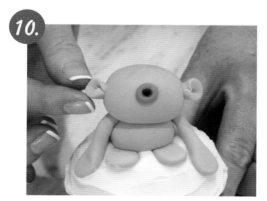

10.

With a toothpick, create an opening on each side of the alien's head and insert the ears.

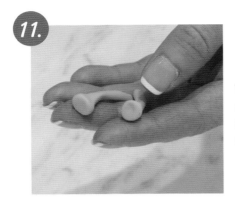

11.

With light green fondant, create 2 short tentacle-like shapes and flatten their ends.

12.

Make 2 holes at the top of the head and insert the tentacles.

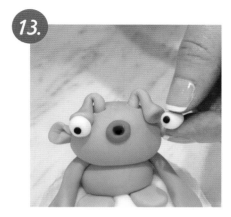

13. Create 2 eyeballs with white fondant, add little black pupils, and place at the flattened end of each tentacle.

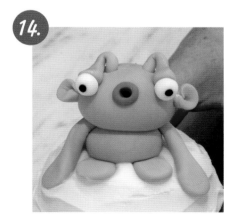

14. The alien is complete!

Funky Monkey

Banana Chocolate Chip Cupcakes with Chocolate Frosting

Go bananas for Funky Monkey! He doesn't have a chip on his shoulder, but he has lots of them — of the chocolate variety — mixed into his banana cupcake!

Makes 12 cupcakes.

INGREDIENTS

For the Cupcakes:
2 ripe bananas

1 cup sugar

2 large eggs

$1/4$ cup plus 2 tablespoons vegetable oil

1 cup all-purpose flour

$1/2$ teaspoon baking soda

1 teaspoon baking powder

Pinch of salt

1 cup semisweet chocolate chips

For the Frosting:
1 cup heavy cream

4 tablespoons unsalted butter

2 tablespoons light corn syrup

10 ounces semisweet chocolate chips

Preheat oven to 350°F (180°C). Place 12 paper baking cups in a muffin pan.

In a large bowl, mash the bananas. Add the sugar and mix well. Then add the eggs and oil and mix well after each addition.

In a small bowl, mix together the flour, baking soda, baking powder, and salt. Add the flour mixture to the banana mixture and stir, being careful not to overmix the batter. Fold in chocolate chips.

Pour the batter into cupcake liners until they are two-thirds full and bake in the center of the oven for 35 minutes or until a wooden toothpick inserted in the center of a cupcake comes out clean. Cool the pan on a rack for 30 minutes before frosting. Store unfrosted cupcakes in an airtight container for up to 3 days.

For the Frosting:

Bring cream, butter, and light corn syrup to a simmer in a medium heavy-bottomed saucepan. Remove from heat and add chocolate chips, mixing until melted and smooth. Whisk occasionally until cool.

Store in refrigerator until ready to frost the cupcakes. If frosting gets too hard, let it sit at room temperature until it's soft enough to spread. The frosting can be stored in a sealed container in the refrigerator for up to 2 days.

You will need:

- Fondant in the following colors: orange, yellow, white, black
- Butter knife
- Toothpick

1.

Spread frosting evenly over the filled cupcake.

2.

With orange fondant, make a pear-shaped ball.

3.

Place on top of the cupcake.

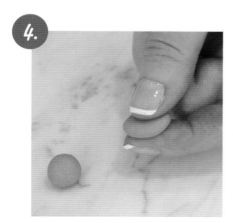

4.

Using more orange fondant, make 2 little balls and flatten them to form the monkey's feet.

5.

Take a smaller amount of yellow fondant, form tiny balls, and flatten them to form the pads of the feet. Place them on the orange feet and use a toothpick to make indentations to form the toes. Place feet as shown.

6.

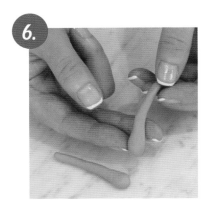

Roll orange fondant into 2 long, thin arms. Flatten them at the end to make the hands.

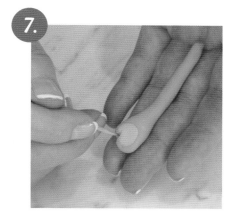

7.

Use a small amount of yellow fondant to create the palms. Place on hands and use a toothpick to create fingers as shown.

8.

Affix the arms at the top of the monkey's body and pose them as shown.

9. With yellow fondant, form a ball and then take about half that amount of orange fondant and form another ball. Place the orange ball at the top back of the yellow ball and place both on the body.

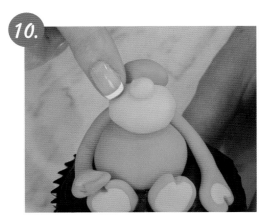

10. Use a tiny amount of yellow fondant to make a round nose and place it on the monkey's face.

Use orange fondant to make 2 balls and flatten them to form the ears. Take a smaller amount of yellow fondant, make 2 flattened balls, and place them in the center of the ears. Use a toothpick to make indentations as shown and place the ears on the sides of the monkey's head.

Make 2 different-sized eyes using white fondant and add little black dots for the pupils. Place them above the nose.

13.

Use a thin strip of yellow fondant to create the eyebrow and gently place it above the eyes.

14.

Use orange fondant to make a small orange ball, affix it to the monkey's face, and use a toothpick to make a hole in the center to form the mouth.

Tako Tentacles

Devil's Food Cupcakes with Mint Mascarpone Frosting and
Chocolate Pudding Filling

Watch Tako Tentacles show off his moves while he rides the
waves — proving that when it comes to dancing on a cupcake, six
tentacles are better than one!

Makes 18 cupcakes.

INGREDIENTS

For the Cupcakes:

3 ounces unsweetened
  chocolate
½ cup unsalted butter
2 cups packed dark brown
  sugar
2 large eggs
2 teaspoons vanilla extract
2 cups all-purpose flour
2 teaspoons baking soda
Pinch of salt
½ cup buttermilk
1 cup boiling water

For the Frosting:

1¼ cups confectioners' sugar
6 tablespoons unsalted butter,
  softened
4 ounces cold mascarpone
¼ teaspoon peppermint
  extract

For the Filling:

Chocolate pudding

Preheat oven to 350°F (180°C). Place 18 baking cups in 2
muffin pans.

Melt chocolate and butter together in a double boiler. In a large bowl, stir together the melted chocolate mixture with the sugar. Add the eggs and vanilla and mix until well blended. In a small bowl, mix the flour, baking soda, and salt. Add about half the flour mixture to the chocolate batter, then add the buttermilk, and then the rest of the flour mixture. Stir gently with a wooden spoon until well blended. Add the boiling water and stir.

Pour the batter into cupcake liners until they are about two-thirds full and bake in the center of the oven for about 20 minutes or until a wooden toothpick inserted in the center of a cupcake comes out clean. Cool on rack for 30 minutes before frosting. Store unfrosted cupcakes in an airtight container in the refrigerator for up to 3 days.

For the Frosting:

In a medium bowl, beat the sugar and butter with an electric mixer on medium speed until light and fluffy. Add the mascarpone and peppermint extract and stir until smooth.

Store in refrigerator until ready to frost the cupcakes. If frosting gets too hard, let it sit at room temperature until it's soft enough to spread. The frosting can be stored in a sealed container in the refrigerator for up to 2 days.

Before frosting the cupcakes, fill them with the chocolate pudding. See page 5 for filling instructions.

You will need:

- Fondant in the following colors: blue, light green, white, black
- Butter knife
- Toothpick

1.

Spread frosting evenly over the filled cupcake.

2.

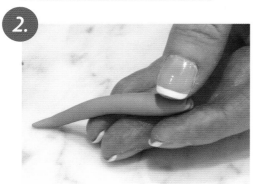

Roll a small amount of blue fondant into a long thin tentacle (about 2 inches long).

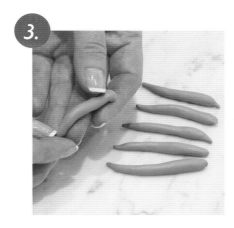

Make 5 more identical tentacles.

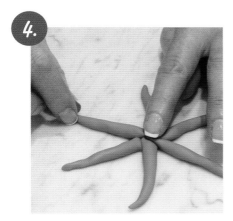

Join the tentacles together at one end to form a star shape.

5.

Lift up the ends a little to create movement as shown, and place little dots of green fondant all over the tentacles.

6.

With blue fondant, make a pear-shaped head.

Add little green dots to the head.

Place the head at the center of the tentacles.

9.

With white fondant, form 2 eyeballs.

10.

Attach the eyes to Tako Tentacles' head.

11.

Take a tiny amount of black fondant to form the pupils and attach to the eyeballs as shown.

12.

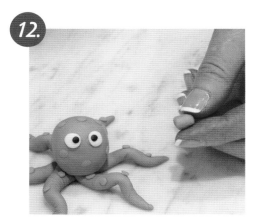

Create a tiny cylinder out of blue fondant and attach it beneath the eyes.

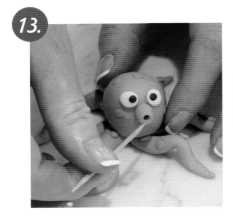

13.

Use a toothpick to make a hole in the center of the cylinder to form the mouth.

14.

Carefully place Tako Tentacles on top of the cupcake.

Miss Molly Mouse

Yellow Cupcakes with Orange Buttercream Frosting and
Orange Marmalade Filling

You could be forgiven for thinking Miss Molly Mouse is the Queen
of Cheese. She has the right teeth for it! She and her precious little
accessories are good enough to eat!

Makes 12 cupcakes.

INGREDIENTS

For the Cupcakes:

1 1/4 cups all-purpose flour
1/2 teaspoon baking soda
1 teaspoon baking powder
Pinch of salt
1/2 cup unsalted butter,
   softened
1 cup sugar
3 large eggs, separated
1 teaspoon vanilla extract
1/2 cup sour cream

For the Frosting:

1 cup unsalted butter,
   softened
4 cups confectioners' sugar
1 teaspoon orange zest
4 tablespoons fresh-
   squeezed orange juice
2 tablespoons light corn syrup
2 teaspoons vanilla extract

For the Filling:

Orange marmalade

Preheat oven to 350°F (180°C). Place 12 baking cups in
muffin pan.

In a medium bowl, mix together flour, baking soda, baking powder, and salt. In a larger bowl, cream butter and sugar together until light and fluffy. Add egg yolks one at a time, reserving the whites in a separate bowl. Mix well after each addition, and then add vanilla. Add the flour mix, alternately with the sour cream. Meanwhile, beat egg whites with an electric mixer on high speed until stiff, and then gently fold into the rest of the batter with a wooden spoon.

Pour the batter into cupcake liners until they are about two-thirds full and bake in the center of the oven for about 20 minutes or until a wooden toothpick inserted in the center of a cupcake comes out clean. Cool on rack for 30 minutes before frosting. Store unfrosted cupcakes in an airtight container for up to 3 days.

For the Frosting:

Cream butter with an electric mixer on medium speed until smooth. Gradually add sugar, one cup at a time. Add orange zest, orange juice, vanilla, and light corn syrup. Beat until light and fluffy.

Store in the refrigerator until ready to frost the cupcakes. If the frosting gets too hard, let it sit at room temperature until it's soft enough to spread. The frosting can be stored in a sealed container in the refrigerator for up to 2 days.

Before frosting the cupcakes, fill them with the orange marmalade. See page 5 for filling instructions.

You will need:

- Fondant in the following colors: red, white, pink, black, orange, yellow
- Butter knife
- Toothpick

1.

Spread frosting evenly over the filled cupcake.

2.

With red fondant, make a large mouse-shaped oval for the body.

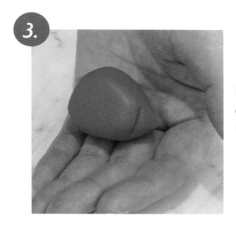

3.

Use the knife to make a small opening for the mouth as shown.

4.

Using a tiny amount of white fondant, make a small flat triangle and make a slit in the middle to create 2 teeth.

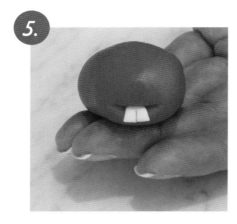

5. Insert the teeth into the mouse's mouth.

6. Place the body on top of the cupcake.

7.

With pink fondant, make a little ball for the nose and place it on the point above the mouth.

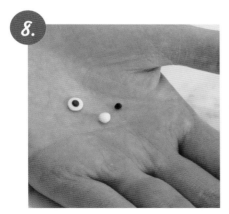

8.

With white and black fondant, create 2 eyes and affix them to the face.

9.

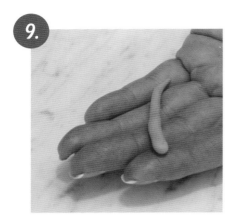

With pink fondant, roll out a long thin tail.

10.

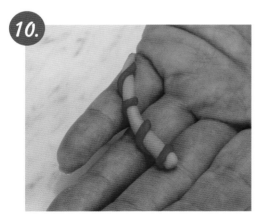

Take a long, even thinner roll of red fondant and wind it around the pink tail.

11.

Use a toothpick to make a hole in the back of the mouse and insert the tail, positioning the end on top of the body as shown.

12.

With red fondant, create 2 large flat circles to form the ears. Use a smaller amount of pink fondant to make 2 flat circles and place them on the red circles as shown.

13.

Pinch the ears at one end and affix them to each side of the head.

14.

With tiny amounts of orange and yellow fondant, make a tiny flower and earrings and place them on the mouse as shown.

Mad Lizard

Pumpkin Cupcakes with Vanilla Buttercream Frosting and Apple Butter Filling

Look at our Mad Lizard languishing on the rocks. Boasting stripes, three googly eyes, and a forked tongue, she dares you to disturb her fiercely guarded treasure!

Makes 12 cupcakes.

INGREDIENTS

For the Cupcakes:
1 cup all-purpose flour
1 cup sugar
1 teaspoon cinnamon
$1/4$ teaspoon nutmeg
$1/4$ teaspoon ground cloves
1 teaspoon baking powder
$1/2$ teaspoon baking soda
Pinch of salt
1 cup solid canned pumpkin (not pumpkin filling)
2 large eggs
$1/4$ cup plus 2 tablespoons vegetable oil

For the Frosting:
1 cup unsalted butter, softened
1 teaspoon vanilla extract
4 cups confectioners' sugar
2 teaspoons milk

For the Filling:
Apple butter

Preheat oven to 350°F (180°C). Place 12 baking cups in muffin pan.

In a large bowl, mix together flour, sugar, cinnamon, nutmeg, cloves, baking powder, baking soda, and salt. In a medium bowl, mix together pumpkin, eggs, and oil. Add the pumpkin mixture to the flour mixture and blend well.

Pour the batter into cupcake liners until they are about two-thirds full and bake in the center of the oven for about 25 minutes or until a wooden toothpick inserted in the center of a cupcake comes out clean. Cool on rack for 30 minutes before frosting. Store unfrosted cupcakes in an airtight container for up to 3 days.

For the Frosting:
Cream butter with an electric mixer in a large bowl. Add vanilla and then gradually add sugar, beating well and scraping the sides of the bowl. Add milk and beat until light and fluffy.

Store in the refrigerator until ready to frost the cupcakes. If the frosting gets too hard, let it sit at room temperature until it's soft enough to spread. The frosting can be stored in a sealed container in the refrigerator for up to 2 days.

Before frosting the cupcakes, fill them with the apple butter. See page 5 for filling instructions.

1.

Spread frosting evenly over the filled cupcake.

2.

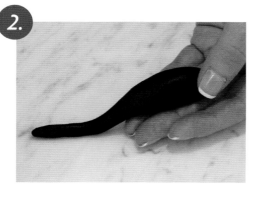

With black fondant, create a long shape to form the body, rolling the end thinner to form the tail.

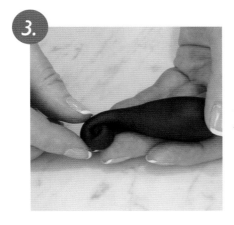

3. Curl the tail around at the end as shown.

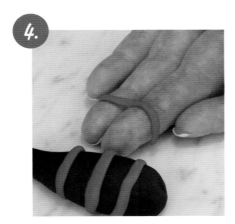

4. Create stripes using little strips of red fondant and secure them to the lizard's body.

5.

Place the body on top of the cupcake.

6.

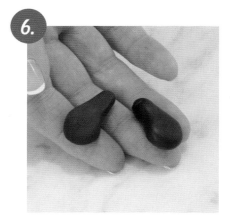

With a little black fondant, create 2 identical back legs as shown.

7.

Using a toothpick, create an indentation in the middle of each foot. Place the back legs on each side of the lizard's body.

8.

Using a small amount of black fondant, create the lizard's front legs; make indentations with the toothpick and affix to the body.

9

With black fondant, create an olive-shaped head.

With a small, sharp knife, create a mouth opening and use a toothpick to add 2 nostrils.

11.

With red fondant, shape a forked tongue and insert it in the lizard's mouth.

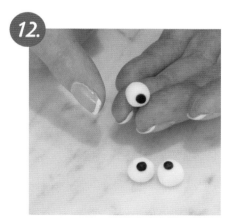

12.

With white fondant, create 3 eyeballs and add a dot of black on each for the pupils.

Place the head on the body and then place the 3 eyeballs on the head, leaving space between them for the eyelids.

To create the eyelids, make thin half-circles of red fondant and wrap them around the top of each eyeball as shown.

Donald Trunk

Yellow Cupcakes with Chocolate Frosting and Strawberry Filling

Who says Donald Trunk is full of hot air? Hot hair, maybe, and lots and lots of bubbles! He sits atop this delicious yellow cupcake guarding his precious stash of strawberries.

Makes 12 cupcakes.

INGREDIENTS

For the Cupcakes:
1 1/4 cups all-purpose flour
1/2 teaspoon baking soda
1 teaspoon baking powder
Pinch of salt
1/2 cup unsalted butter, softened
1 cup sugar
3 large eggs, separated
1 teaspoon vanilla extract
1/2 cup sour cream

For the Frosting:
1 cup heavy cream
4 tablespoons unsalted butter
2 tablespoons light corn syrup
10 ounces semisweet chocolate chips

For the Filling:
Fresh strawberries, thinly diced

Preheat oven to 350°F (180°C). Place 12 baking cups in muffin pan.

In a medium bowl, mix together flour, baking soda, baking powder, and salt. In a larger bowl, cream butter and sugar together until light and fluffy. Add egg yolks one at a time, reserving the whites in a separate bowl. Mix well after each addition, and then add vanilla. Add the flour mix, alternately with the sour cream. Meanwhile, beat egg whites with an electric mixer on high speed until stiff, and then gently fold into the rest of the batter with a wooden spoon.

Pour the batter into cupcake liners until they are about two-thirds full and bake in the center of the oven for about 20 minutes or until a wooden toothpick inserted in the center of a cupcake comes out clean. Cool on rack for 30 minutes before frosting. Store unfrosted cupcakes in an airtight container for up to 3 days.

For the Frosting:

Bring cream, butter, and light corn syrup to a simmer in a medium, heavy-bottomed saucepan. Remove from heat and add chocolate chips, mixing until melted and smooth. Whisk occasionally until cool. Store in the refrigerator until ready to frost the cupcakes. If the frosting gets too hard, let it sit out at room temperature until it's soft enough to spread. The frosting can be stored in a sealed container in the refrigerator for up to 2 days.

Before frosting the cupcakes, fill them with the diced strawberries. See page 5 for filling instructions.

You will need:

- Fondant in the following colors: gray, white, black, orange
- Butter knife
- Small, sharp knife
- Toothpick

1.

Spread frosting evenly over the filled cupcake.

2.

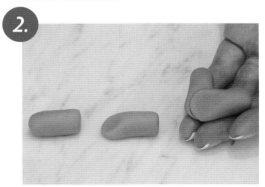

With gray fondant, roll 2 small cylinders to form the back legs. Press down on one end of each cylinder and then press these ends together as shown.

3.

Roll a ball of gray fondant into an oval shape to create the elephant's body. Press the large end of the oval onto the feet where they're pressed together.

4.

For the front legs, use gray fondant to roll 2 small cylinders similar to the ones created for the back legs. Press the front legs to the front of the body.

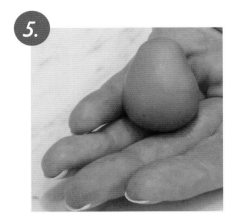

5.

With half as much gray fondant as used for the body, roll a pear-shaped head.

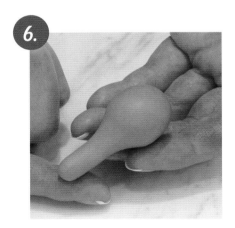

6.

Roll the small end of the pear shape to form a cylinder (the elephant's trunk).

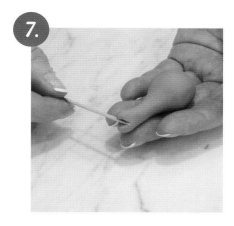

7.

Flatten the end of the trunk
and use a toothpick to
create an indentation
as shown.

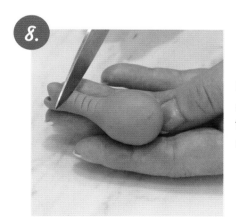

8.

Use a small, sharp knife to
create indentations on the
top of the trunk in order to
create a wrinkle effect.

9.

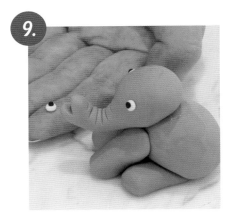

Firmly secure the head to the body and position the trunk as shown. Add 2 eyes using white and black fondant.

10.

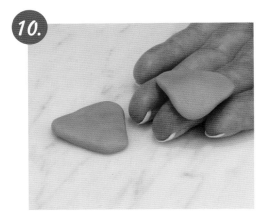

With gray fondant, create 2 identical flat triangle-like shapes.

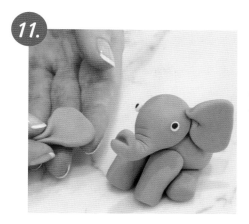

11.

Pinch one end of each triangle between your fingers and attach to each side of the elephant's head.

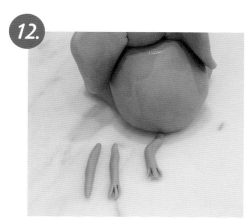

12.

With gray fondant, roll a tiny, thin cylinder to form the tail. Use a sharp knife to create indentations at the end and attach the tail to the elephant as shown.

13.

With orange fondant, form a flat rectangle and use a small, sharp knife to create slits in the long side as shown. This is the elephant's hair.

14.

Place the hair on top of the head by attaching the unslit side and curling the other portion over as shown. Place the finished elephant on top of the cupcake.

Howl Owl

Yellow Cupcakes with Lemon Buttercream Frosting and Lemon Curd Filling

Whoooooo goes there? These three little owls stand guard over their forest domain. Why are they howling? Could it be they ate too much of their lemon curd filling?

Makes 12 cupcakes.

INGREDIENTS

For the Cupcakes:
1 ¼ cups all-purpose flour
½ teaspoon baking soda
1 teaspoon baking powder
Pinch of salt
½ cup unsalted butter, softened
1 cup sugar
3 large eggs, separated
1 teaspoon vanilla extract
½ cup sour cream

For the Frosting:
1 cup unsalted butter, softened
4 cups confectioners' sugar
1 ½ teaspoons lemon zest
2 teaspoons vanilla extract
2 tablespoons light corn syrup

For the Filling:
Lemon curd

Preheat oven to 350°F (180°C). Place 12 baking cups in muffin pan.

In a medium bowl, mix together flour, baking soda, baking powder, and salt. In a larger bowl, cream butter and sugar together until light and fluffy. Add egg yolks one at a time, reserving the whites in a separate bowl. Mix well after each addition, and then add vanilla. Add the flour mix, alternately with the sour cream. Meanwhile, beat egg whites with an electric mixer on high speed until stiff, and then gently fold into the rest of the batter with a wooden spoon.

Pour the batter into cupcake liners until they are about two-thirds full and bake in the center of the oven for about 20 minutes or until a wooden toothpick inserted in the center of a cupcake comes out clean. Cool on rack for 30 minutes before frosting. Store unfrosted cupcakes in an airtight container for up to 3 days.

For the Frosting:
Cream butter with an electric mixer on medium speed until smooth. Gradually add sugar, one cup at a time. Add lemon zest, vanilla, and light corn syrup. Beat until light and fluffy. Store in the refrigerator until ready to frost the cupcakes. If the frosting gets too hard, let it sit out at room temperature until it's soft enough to spread. The frosting can be stored in a sealed container in the refrigerator for up to 2 days.

Before frosting the cupcakes, fill them with the lemon curd. See page 5 for filling instructions.

You will need:

- Fondant in the following colors: light purple, dark purple, white, black, orange
- Butter knife
- Small, sharp knife
- Toothpick

1.

Spread frosting evenly over the filled cupcake.

2.

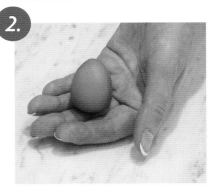

With light purple fondant, roll an oval shape to form the owl's body.

3. With a small amount of dark purple fondant, create a flat triangle.

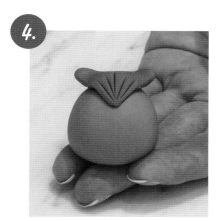

4. Press the triangle on top of the owl's body and pull corners up slightly to form ear tips. Use a sharp knife to add indentations as shown.

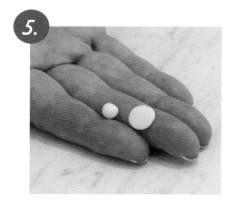

With white fondant, roll 2 small balls and flatten them to form the owl's eyes.

Using black fondant, roll 2 tiny pupils, add them to the white eyes, and place them on the owl's face.

7.

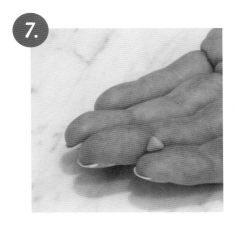

With a tiny amount of orange fondant, roll a cone shape to form the beak.

8.

Place the beak on the owl's face as shown.

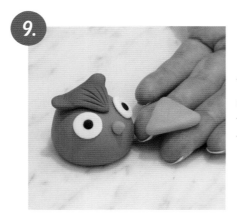

9.

To form the feet, take a small amount of orange fondant and make a flat triangle.

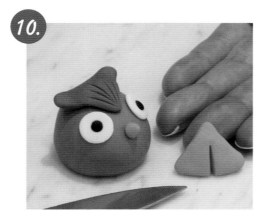

10.

With a sharp knife, cut a slit in the middle of the triangle to form 2 feet.

11.

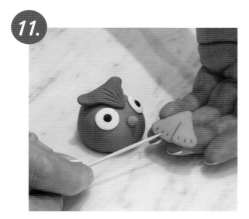

Use a toothpick to make indentations for the toes.

12.

Place the body on top of the feet as shown.

With dark purple fondant, roll a small ball and flatten it to create a circle.

With a sharp knife, cut the circle in half to create 2 wings and place them on each side of the body as shown. Place the finished owl on top of the cupcake.

Cheeky Chickie

Banana Cupcakes with Chocolate Frosting and Peanut Butter Filling

This little chickie thinks she's a rubber duckie. Sorry, Cheeky Chickie, but the orange mohawk gives you away every time! And so does that nutty-flavored peanut butter filling!

Makes 12 cupcakes.

INGREDIENTS

For the Cupcakes:
2 ripe bananas
1 cup sugar
2 large eggs
$1/4$ cup plus 2 tablespoons vegetable oil
1 cup all-purpose flour
$1/2$ teaspoon baking soda
1 teaspoon baking powder
Pinch of salt

For the Frosting:
1 cup heavy cream
4 tablespoons unsalted butter
2 tablespoons light corn syrup
10 ounces semisweet chocolate chips

For the Filling:
Creamy peanut butter

Preheat oven to 350°F (180°C). Place 12 paper baking cups in a muffin pan.

In a large bowl, mash the bananas. Add the sugar and mix well. Then add the eggs and oil and mix well after each addition. In a small bowl, mix together the flour, baking soda, baking powder, and salt. Add the flour mixture to the banana mixture and stir, being careful not to overmix the batter.

Pour the batter into cupcake liners until they are two-thirds full and bake in the center of the oven for 35 minutes or until a wooden toothpick inserted in the center of a cupcake comes out clean. Cool the pan on a rack for 30 minutes before frosting. Store unfrosted cupcakes in an airtight container for up to 3 days.

For the Frosting:

Bring cream, butter, and light corn syrup to a simmer in a medium, heavy-bottomed saucepan. Remove from heat and add chocolate chips, mixing until melted and smooth. Whisk occasionally until cool. Store in the refrigerator until ready to frost the cupcakes. If the frosting gets too hard, let it sit out at room temperature until it's soft enough to spread. The frosting can be stored in a sealed container in the refrigerator for up to 2 days.

Before frosting the cupcakes, fill them with the peanut butter. See page 5 for filling instructions.

You will need:

- Fondant in the following colors:
  yellow, orange, white, black
- Butter knife
- Small, sharp knife
- Toothpick

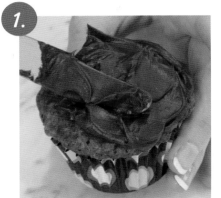

1.

Spread frosting evenly over
the filled cupcake.

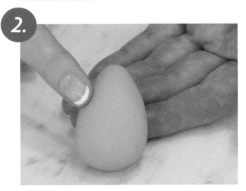

2.

With yellow fondant,
roll a pear-shaped
body.

3.

Slightly pinch the narrow end of the body to form the tail feathers and make some indentations with a toothpick as shown.

4.

Roll a small ball of yellow fondant to form the head.

5.

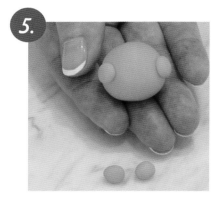

Roll 2 tiny balls of yellow fondant to form the cheeks and place them on each side of the head.

6.

With a toothpick, place an indentation on each cheek as shown.

7.

With orange fondant, roll a small ball and flatten between your fingers to make a circle.

8.

Cut the circle in half with a knife and connect the 2 half circles to form an open beak.

9.

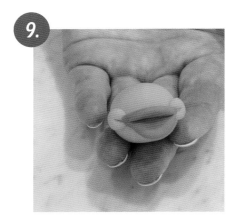

Place the beak between the cheeks as shown.

10.

With white fondant, make 2 flattened eyes and place them above the beak. With black fondant, make 2 black dots for pupils and place them on the white.

11. With orange fondant, form 2 triangles for the chickie's feet and place them on the cupcake as shown.

12. Place the head on the chickie's body and then the body on the feet as shown.

13.

With yellow fondant, form 2 tear-shaped wings, add indentations with a toothpick, and place on either side of the body as shown.

14.

With orange fondant, form a small flat square and cut slits on one side with a sharp knife. Place the uncut side on top of the head to form a mohawk.

Whamburger

Devil's Food Cupcakes with Orange Buttercream Frosting and Vanilla Pudding Filling

Beware the Whamburger! If you're not careful, he'll steal all your french fries and maybe even your milkshake! Don't worry though. Deep inside he's a real softie — with a vanilla pudding filling.

Makes 18 cupcakes.

INGREDIENTS

For the Cupcakes:

3 ounces unsweetened chocolate

$\frac{1}{2}$ cup unsalted butter

2 cups packed dark brown sugar

2 large eggs

2 teaspoons vanilla extract

2 cups all-purpose flour

2 teaspoons baking soda

Pinch of salt

$\frac{1}{2}$ cup buttermilk

1 cup boiling water

For the Frosting:

1 cup unsalted butter, softened

4 cups confectioners' sugar

1 teaspoon orange zest

4 tablespoons fresh-squeezed orange juice

2 tablespoons light corn syrup

2 teaspoons vanilla extract

For the Filling:

Vanilla pudding

Preheat oven to 350°F (180°C). Place 18 baking cups in 2 muffin pans.

Melt chocolate and butter together in a double boiler. In a large bowl, stir together the melted chocolate mixture with the sugar. Add the eggs and vanilla and mix until well blended. In a small bowl, mix the flour, baking soda, and salt. Add about half the flour mixture to the chocolate batter, then add the buttermilk, and then the rest of the flour mixture. Stir gently with a wooden spoon until well blended. Add the boiling water and stir.

Pour the batter into cupcake liners until they are about two-thirds full and bake in the center of the oven for about 20 minutes or until a wooden toothpick inserted in the center of a cupcake comes out clean. Cool on rack for 30 minutes before frosting. Store unfrosted cupcakes in an airtight container for up to 3 days.

For the Frosting:

Cream butter with an electric mixer on medium speed until smooth. Gradually add sugar, one cup at a time. Add orange zest, orange juice, vanilla, and light corn syrup. Beat until light and fluffy. Store in the refrigerator until ready to frost the cupcakes. If the frosting gets too hard, let it sit out at room temperature until it's soft enough to spread. The frosting can be stored in a sealed container in the refrigerator for up to 2 days.

Before frosting the cupcakes, fill them with the vanilla pudding. See page 5 for filling instructions.

You will need:

- Fondant in the following colors: light brown, mustard yellow, red, dark brown, green, tan, white, black
- Butter knife
- Toothpick

1.

Spread frosting evenly over the filled cupcake.

2.

With light brown fondant, roll 2 round balls and flatten them to form 2 bun shapes as shown.

3.

Place the bottom bun on the cupcake.

4.

With mustard yellow fondant, form 2 drool shapes and attach to the sides of the bun as shown.

5.

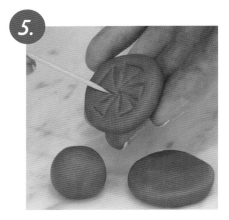

With red fondant, roll a small ball and flatten it to create a tomato slice. For more detail, use a toothpick to create triangle indentations as shown.

6.

Place the tomato slice on the bun as shown. It should be hanging over the bun slightly so it looks like the whamburger's tongue is sticking out.

7.

With dark brown fondant, roll a ball and flatten it to make the patty. Place on top of the bun as shown, allowing the tomato to protrude beneath it.

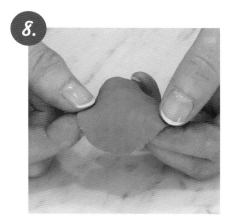

8.

With green fondant, roll a ball and flatten it until it is quite thin, pressing it around the sides to make it look like lettuce.

9.

Place the lettuce on top of the patty and then place the top bun on top of the lettuce as shown.

10.

With tan fondant, create tiny sesame seeds and place around the top of the bun.

With white fondant, roll 2 small balls to form the eyes and place them on the bun as shown.

With black fondant, roll 2 smaller balls and flatten them to form the pupils. Add them to the eyeballs so the whamburger appears a little demented.

13.

With light brown fondant, roll a small ball and flatten it. Use a knife to cut it in half to create eyelids.

14.

Place the eyelids over the eyeballs as shown.

Deucie Brucie

Pumpkin Ginger Cupcakes with Green Tea Frosting

It's a grand slam for these three tennis balls. They may look a little worse for wear, but they're always game for another match. Their secret? A powerful serve and super crystallized ginger.

Makes 12 cupcakes.

INGREDIENTS

For the Cupcakes:
1 cup all-purpose flour
1 cup sugar
1 teaspoon cinnamon
$1/4$ teaspoon nutmeg
$1/4$ teaspoon ground cloves
1 teaspoon baking powder
$1/2$ teaspoon baking soda
Pinch of salt
1 cup solid canned pumpkin
   (not pumpkin filling)
2 large eggs
$1/4$ cup plus 2 tablespoons
   vegetable oil
2 tablespoons thinly diced
   crystallized ginger

For the Frosting:
1 cup unsalted butter,
   softened
1 teaspoon vanilla extract
4 cups confectioners' sugar
2 teaspoons milk
2 teaspoons green tea
   powder, or to taste
$1/2$ teaspoon cardamom
   powder, or to taste

Preheat oven to 350°F (180°C). Place 12 baking cups in muffin pan.

In a large bowl, mix together flour, sugar, cinnamon, nutmeg, cloves, baking powder, baking soda, and salt. In a medium bowl, mix together pumpkin, eggs, and oil. Add the pumpkin mixture to the flour mixture and mix until blended. Stir in the crystallized ginger.

Pour the batter into cupcake liners until they are about two-thirds full and bake in the center of the oven for about 25 minutes or until a wooden toothpick inserted in the center of a cupcake comes out clean. Cool on rack for 30 minutes before frosting. Store unfrosted cupcakes in an airtight container for up to 3 days.

For the Frosting:

Cream butter in a large bowl with an electric mixer. Add vanilla. Gradually add sugar, beating well and scraping down the sides of the bowl. Add milk and continue beating until light and fluffy. Add green tea and cardamom powders and beat until thoroughly blended.

Store in the refrigerator until ready to frost the cupcakes. If the frosting gets too hard, let it sit out at room temperature until it's soft enough to spread. The frosting can be stored in a sealed container in the refrigerator for up to 2 days.

You will need:

- Fondant in the following colors: yellow, white, black, pink, beige
- Butter knife
- Small, sharp knife
- Toothpick

Spread frosting evenly over the cupcake.

With yellow fondant, roll a big ball.

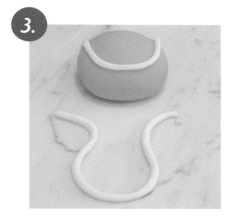

3. Roll a piece of white fondant into a long string and place it in a curved manner around the top of the ball as shown.

4. With a small amount of white fondant, create 2 large eyeballs and place them on the ball.

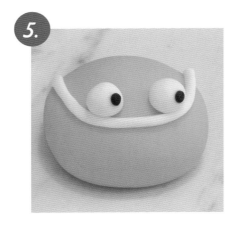

With a tiny amount of black fondant, create 2 pupils and place them on the eyeballs.

6

To create the eyelids, roll a small amount of yellow fondant into a ball and flatten it.

7. Cut the flattened circle in half with a knife and drape each half over an eyeball as shown.

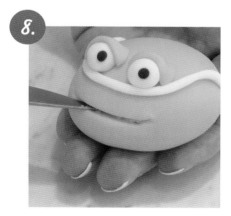

8. With a sharp knife, create a mouth opening. You can create any expression you like.

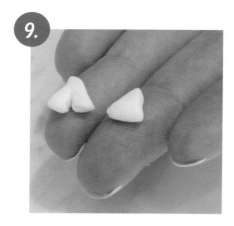

9.

For the teeth, create a small flat triangle out of white fondant and cut a slit in the middle with a sharp knife.

10.

Affix the teeth to the mouth as shown.

11.

To add a tongue, use pink fondant to form a small cylinder. Flatten the cylinder and use a toothpick to make an indentation in the middle.

12.

Insert the tongue in the tennis ball's mouth.

13.

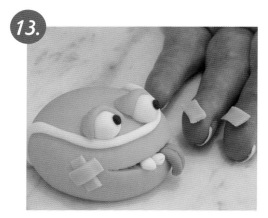

With beige or flesh-colored fondant, form 2 flattened rectangles and place them on the tennis ball in a crisscross manner (to create a Band-Aid).

14.

Place the tennis ball on the cupcake. Use your imagination to create as many facial expressions as you like.

Swishy Fishy

Banana Cupcakes with Vanilla Buttercream Frosting and Strawberry Jam Filling

Those lips, those eyes, those orange spots! This swishy fishy is a dream come true as she gets ready for her fish tank close-up. As if that's not enough, she tempts us with her sweet strawberry jam filling!

Makes 12 cupcakes.

INGREDIENTS

For the Cupcakes:
2 ripe bananas
1 cup sugar
2 large eggs
$\frac{1}{4}$ cup plus 2 tablespoons vegetable oil
1 cup all-purpose flour
$\frac{1}{2}$ teaspoon baking soda
1 teaspoon baking powder
Pinch of salt

For the Frosting:
1 cup unsalted butter, softened
1 teaspoon vanilla extract
4 cups confectioners' sugar
2 teaspoons milk

For the Filling:
Strawberry jam

Preheat oven to 350°F (180°C). Place 12 paper baking cups in a muffin pan.

In a large bowl, mash the bananas. Add the sugar and mix well. Then add the eggs and oil and mix well after each addition. In a small bowl, mix together the flour, baking soda, baking powder, and salt. Add the flour mixture to the banana mixture and stir, being careful not to overmix the batter.

Pour the batter into cupcake liners until they are two-thirds full and bake in the center of the oven for 35 minutes or until a wooden toothpick inserted in the center of a cupcake comes out clean. Cool the pan on a rack for 30 minutes before frosting. Store unfrosted cupcakes in an airtight container for up to 3 days.

For the Frosting:

Cream butter with an electric mixer in a large bowl. Add vanilla and then gradually add sugar, beating well and scraping the sides of the bowl. Add milk and beat until light and fluffy. Store in the refrigerator until ready to frost the cupcakes. If the frosting gets too hard, let it sit out at room temperature until it's soft enough to spread. The frosting can be stored in a sealed container in the refrigerator for up to 2 days.

Before frosting the cupcakes, fill them with the strawberry jam. See page 5 for filling instructions.

You will need:

- Fondant in the following colors: red, orange, white, black, green, blue
- Butter knife
- Small, sharp knife
- Toothpick

1.

Spread frosting evenly over the filled cupcake.

2.

With red fondant, roll a pear-shaped oval to form the body.

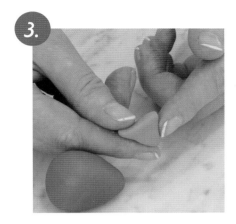

With orange fondant, sculpt a triangle to create the tail.

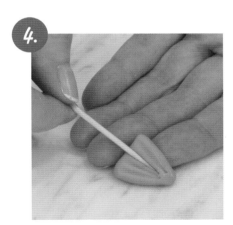

Use a toothpick to add indentations to the tail as shown.

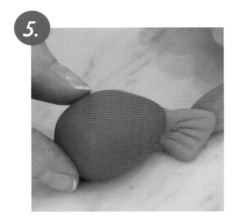

5. Attach the tail to the body, bending it slightly to make it look like it's swishing.

6. Roll a small amount of orange fondant in a full lip shape to create the mouth. Affix it to the face.

7.

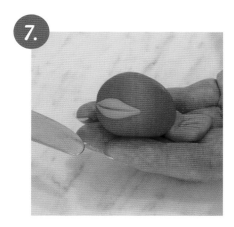

Use a sharp knife to make a slit to create the mouth opening.

8.

With white fondant, create 2 small balls for the eyes. Add tiny dots of black fondant to the white balls to form pupils.

9.

Affix the eyes to the sides of the face as shown.

10.

Roll a small amount of orange fondant into a ball, flatten it into a very thin circle, and cut it in half with a sharp knife to create 2 eyelids.

11.

Affix the eyelids over the eyes as shown.

12.

Decorate the body using little balls of orange fondant. Place the fish on the cupcake.

13. Take a small amount of orange fondant and flatten it in a triangle shape to form the fin. Use a toothpick to make indentations. Place the fin on top of the fish.

14. With green and blue fondant, roll tiny irregularly shaped balls for rocks and place them around the fish.

Dino-Mite

Yellow Cupcakes with White Chocolate Chips and Green Tea Frosting

Dinosaurs and dynamite — what a dynamic duo! And this sweet little guy is filled with white chocolate chips. Please don't play with fire, Dino-Mite. The results could be explosive!

Makes 12 cupcakes.

INGREDIENTS

For the Cupcakes:
1 1/4 cups all-purpose flour
1/2 teaspoon baking soda
1 teaspoon baking powder
Pinch of salt
1/2 cup unsalted butter, softened
1 cup sugar
3 large eggs, separated
1 teaspoon vanilla extract
1/2 cup sour cream
1 cup white chocolate chips

For the Frosting:
1 cup unsalted butter, softened
1 teaspoon vanilla extract
4 cups confectioners' sugar
2 teaspoons milk
2 teaspoons green tea powder, or to taste
1/2 teaspoon cardamom powder, or to taste

Preheat oven to 350°F (180°C). Place 12 paper baking cups in a muffin pan.

In a medium bowl, mix together flour, baking soda, baking powder, and salt. In a larger bowl, cream butter and sugar together until light and fluffy. Add egg yolks one at a time, reserving the whites in a separate bowl. Mix well after each addition, and then add vanilla. Add the flour mix, alternately with the sour cream. Meanwhile, beat egg whites with an electric mixer on high speed until stiff, and then gently fold into the rest of the batter with a wooden spoon. Gently stir in 1 cup of white chocolate chips.

Pour the batter into cupcake liners until they are about two-thirds full and bake in the center of the oven for about 20 minutes or until a wooden toothpick inserted in the center of a cupcake comes out clean. Cool on rack for 30 minutes before frosting. Store unfrosted cupcakes in an airtight container for up to 3 days.

For the Frosting:

Cream butter in a large bowl with an electric mixer. Add vanilla. Gradually add sugar, beating well and scraping down the sides of the bowl. Add milk and continue beating until light and fluffy. Add green tea and cardamom powders and beat until thoroughly blended.

Store in the refrigerator until ready to frost the cupcakes. If the frosting gets too hard, let it sit at room temperature until it's soft enough to spread. The frosting can be stored in a sealed container in the refrigerator for up to 2 days.

You will need:

- Fondant in the following colors: green, purple, white, black, red
- Butter knife
- Toothpick

1.

Spread frosting evenly over the cupcake.

2.

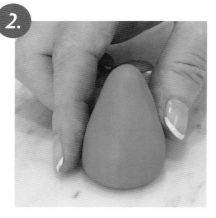

With green fondant, roll a ball to form a cone shape.

3.

Lengthen the pointed side to form a tail and pose it as shown.

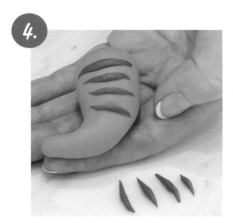

4.

With purple fondant, roll 4 small strips to form stripes and place them on the dinosaur's back.

Add little dots of purple fondant to decorate the dinosaur's tail.

For the dinosaur's back legs, use green fondant to create 2 small logs and flatten one end of each. At the other end, use a toothpick to make indentations to create the claws.

7.

For the arms, repeat the above process using a smaller amount of green fondant.

8.

Place the legs and arms on each side of the body as shown.

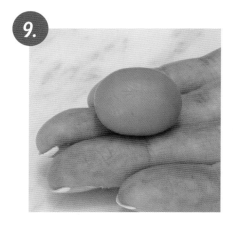

9.

Roll a small ball of green fondant to form the head.

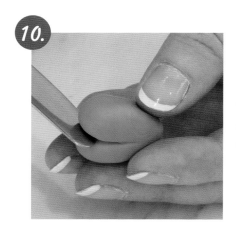

10.

With a knife, create an opening for the mouth as shown.

11.

Place the head on top of the body and use a toothpick to add nostrils.

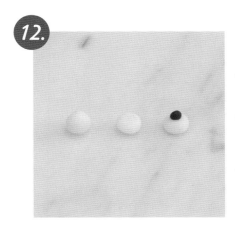

12.

With white fondant, roll 2 little balls to form the eyes and place them on the head. Add tiny dots of black fondant to the eyes to form the pupils.